INFAMOUS-INK PUBLISHING
9116 E. Sprague Ave., #604
Spokane Valley WA, 99206

Cover Design by Summer Webster and John Steiner

Printed in cooperation with
American Artists Incorporated, and Infamous-Ink
Publishing.

Edited by Kathy Hammond

POEMS FROM THE INNER SOUL

BY L.J. HOPE

ACKNOWLEDGEMENTS

I want to thank my publisher, Kathy, for a dream come true. And I want to thank Skin for pointing me in the right direction. If it wasn't for these two people, it would never happen.

I'd like to thank Katie Willis and Burdock Book Collective out of Alabama who set me up with prison advocates. And to Re'n'ee Welsh who is a prison advocate and now my friend. Enjoy your retirement. Karen Cain for her help with info. And my dear friend, Summer Webster, for helping me with the cover. You're awesome!

Also, to Prison Covid Magazine for info on Covid and the budget. To Prison Book Program, c/o Lucy Parson Bookstore, for books and info. The Prisoners Literature, c/o Bound Together Books for books and info. And College Guild out of Maine for helping me and prisoners around the U.S. for keeping our educational juices flowing for free.

A special thank you to Pat and Dan Deardorff. Thanks for everything and for being my lifetime friends. And I want to thank you all, for what's happening is effecting all our souls.

DEDICATION

I dedicate this book to my kids and their kids, and to my incarcerated Brothers and Sisters in the U.S. and around the world.

This is to all our kids, fathers, brothers, sisters, wives, and husbands. That the business is taken out of prison and remember we all are humane. You could be the next slave.

FORWARD

This book of poems comes from the soul, and will give you the insight on what's going on in Washington State Prisons, and around the U.S.

Hopefully, some of these poems will touch your heart and soul, knowing what's really going on in prisons.

CONTENTS

INTRODUCTION

PRISONS OF THE U.S.

They teach you all through the New World that slavery is wrong and inhumane. But, yet the whole of the United States still have slaves. With lives still being mistreated, there's still abuse. They stopped the hangings and the whippings, but now they abuse verbally, mentally, by bad food, Solitary, little movement, and you have to work for pennies with hands on abuse.

And it's not just one race, it's all races. Lots of money is made by the states. The Slave Master gets paid millions to hire slave masters to keep slaves coming in. The business is still going on and thriving.

If there is any quality of life, the slaves have to pay for it at double to triple prices. Remember, they still have slave wages, and the slave masters make a profit off everything including their lives.

You can watch while they stumble, while still in chains. Looks like bad habits are hard to break over a century old and going.

13th AMENDMENT, (1865)

In 1865, the United States Constitution passed the 13th Amendment saying slavery is abolished except in prisons.

Slavery is alive and well with the abuse they apply and the money they make for turning prisons into businesses. You can buy stocks and bonds in correctional industries, and other money-making programs they use prisons for. While over taxing of the slaves and paying them next to nothing but pennies, and if they don't do this there is punishment. Slavery has never been abolished, and one day it can be you or your kids, a family member or loved ones.

From 1865 to 2024
Slavery, alive and well.

WHAT'S GOING ON IN WASHINGTON STATE

Congressman: Makes $174,000.00 a year, to make laws.

The Democrats say they want to empty prisons and enforce sentence reform. They say this to our friends and families, and we need your votes, and we will make this happen. They put in Legislative Bills that would help the incarcerated and their families, but when it comes to the votes to make this happen, they will vote for the least one that will help little. The major ones that will help say we will do this next year. They keep doing this and nothing happens, and again they want your votes.

The Republicans just want to lock you and throw away the key. But what they both have in common is they really don't want to stop mass incarceration. They make way too much money, stocks, bonds and all the programs they put together to make money. If they could find a way to make money by emptying prisons? This will never happen. Too much love of Power.

Our prison system is so bad, and the number one reason is the Teamsters union. It is the biggest union in the U.S. In its union are Corrections, Department of Corrections, from jails to the police. With this union that is in charge it allows their union workers to literally get away with crimes: murders, rapes, staff misconducts, sexual abuse of inmates and their coworkers.

In Washington State, this is a regular thing that happens. We have correctional officers who rape inmates in prisons and on
 the streets. When the Department of Corrections finds out, they may not do anything? Most of the time they just move them to another facility and when it keeps happening, they may them off for awhile until things cool down! And if gotten out of control and the media finally gets a hold of it, they get fired but until that happens the union makes DOC hire these people back 5 to 6 times, or more. Then when arrested and tried and found guilty of whatever crime (rape, murder, physical abuse, etc.), when the average citizen would get 20 to life, but correctional officers/police would only get a year in prison. But they don't go to prison, not for a year sentence. They usually go home and continue doing what they have been.

This has been in Washington State media for years, letting the public know what's been going on. The media doesn't care about prisons. These people are doing this to our citizens and not caring about the incarcerated, or what happens to them!

The union is so powerful, they let the union workers hurt, kill and abuse, as long as the union wages are paid. DOC only hires these kinds of people. Many times worse than the incarcerated, and it's a "good ol' boy" system. Prison is a scary place, and it's not from the incarcerated who live there, it's the DOC employees they hired. With these kind of people removed from our system, prisons would be safer and cared about and to have families involved and realize we all are human.

Prisons are such a big moneymaker, as you will read in some of these poems. The sad thing is the fault should go on all of our Governors. They are the Department of Corrections. They know what's going on and they can stop all this abuse, but it's the money and the power that makes them all corrupt, and in their mind above the law.

MY OPINION

Since the Governor is the Head of State, he knows what's going on in prisons and around the states. And, since he's really the person, head of prisons and he hires these people. So every time there is a killing, or death by medical neglect; or by DOC staff; a rape or any kind of violence by DOC employee; or just plain neglect, the Governor should hold the responsibility and be charged with homicide, murder, rape, neglect and so forth.

If this was to happen, we would have none of these problems in prisons. We would have safe and well ran prisons where families and friends would be welcomed and treated with respect when they come to visit! To know that our moms, dads, sisters, brothers, and kids are treated with respect, and to know their incarcerated loved ones are living in a safe and healthy, humane condition, and where Society will welcome them back and help them move forward in life, as it should be.

Everyone makes mistakes, it doesn't give the governors the right to treat humans as slaves! To treat people so bad! They treat the incarcerated worse than animals.

As is, nobody is held accountable for anything.

SLAVERY AT ITS BEST

Slavery at its best,
Stocks and bonds,
Slavery at its best,
Judges, lawyers, movie stars.

In today's correction industries,
Billions made while the slaves get pennies,
Slavery at its best,
Major business, nationwide.

Slavery was abolished,
Except for prisons,
Slavery at its best,
Constitution says it's OK.

Nobody knows, nobody cares,
Judges, lawyers own our jails and prisons,
They prosecute you to the max,
To keep their business in the billions.

Slavery at its best.

BORDER TO FREEDOM

Just wanting a better life,
Hungry and ragged,
From abuse to pain.

The coyotes are howling,
Never a straight line,
A lifetime of imprisonment.

All over dollars,
To see my family,
To see my home.

Tired of being alone,
Overcrowded, nowhere to go,
I see the mountains; I see the stars.

Just to cross over,
Just to go home,
With freedom we all deserve.

If I could be a bird.

CHANGE

Who am I,
Do I really know,
Change is like the seasons.

One day at a time,
You can't change the past,
But the future will tell.

Change is on its way,
If you let it stay,
If you find the path.

You will never stray,
There will be many tsars,
Along the way.

Caring is a start,
If you lead by the heart,
The old ways,
Will never be the same,
The past was never the way,
Change is on the way.

THE FORGOTTEN PEOPLE

Lost, gone, forgotten,
Nobody knows,
They say we deserve what we get,
Animals get treated better.

Many more to come,
You never hear what goes on,
And never will,
Paid media, Senators, Governors.

They all wake up with smiles,
Looking forward to another day,
They say the slave master is dead,
Little do they know!

No one knows and no one cares,
Forgotten people are only a myth,
Does anyone hear what goes on,
I don't think so.

The pain, the tears, the lonely cries,
The forgotten people that nobody knows,
Another day goes,
No future or past.

A mother's lost,
A State's gain,
No end, only a beginning.

RECIDIVISM

Pain is a endless water fall,
Recidivism is a made-up word for the rich,
Legal slavery is in the $ millions,
Greedy smiles in the light of the night.

The tears of my babies,
A heart that will never mend,
No light at the end of the tunnel,
39 years, 0.42 cents.

Disagreements is a punishment,
If you ask why?
"You are not one of us" I was told,
As the everyday abuse goes on.

Can't you read the signs?
Wallets are padded every day,
Nobody knows,
We would be dead if it wasn't for the money.

Slavery is alive and well,
Where it started nobody knows,
Millions is paid to make billions,
They will let the worst of the worst out.

Knowing they will come back,
The ones who won't come back,
They make it so hard they're made to come back.

It's like falling and never hitting the ground,
The heart is sad by the treatment we all had,
And they call this America as we start over again,
Slavery live and well.

DO YOU REMEMBER

Do you remember,
When you say slavery is wrong?
Do you remember,
When you said you won't lie?

Do you remember,
When the food was so bad you couldn't eat it?
Do you remember,
When you said were all equal?

REFLECTIONS

It's like watching a old time movie from the past,
But in the future.
What happen then,
Is true today.

It's looking in a mirror,
And seeing your reflection.
The days that are gone,
Are still here today.

My tears I felt of yesterday,
The gathering as the whips watch.
In my dreams I smell cotton,
As the tears cry me to sleep at night.

My money the Master makes,
The belittling of everything.
The missing of my children,
Hands held empty.

Freedom is a headstone high,
The empty well smiles.
Chained to life,
Today's reflections.

A SAD DAY

I reach down inside,
Just to live one day.
Another friend in a body bag goes by,
A sad day.

The neglect that is so wrong,
Taking pleasure
In the discomfort of others.
Causing death with no countability.

Another chapter in my life,
Life is so short.
One day at a time,
The abuse is so insane.

NEVER'S FOREVER

My heart is trapped inside,
Another day of nothing,
Like the crashing tides.
Never's forever.

BUT WE WANT THE MONEY MORE

We want sentence reform,
But we want the money more.
We want to empty prisons,
But we want the money more.

The power and the money,
Like none other.
Business of abuse,
But we want the money more.

Bare minimum we give,
But we want the money more.
More the better,
But we want the money more.

We don't care about the lives we hurt,
But we want the money more.
Billions for us,
Pennies for you.

We don't pay the bills,
The state does.
Hands wide open,
But we want the money more.

CLEMENCY

To help the rehabilitated,
To give hope,
To stop the tears,
Give chances.

Understanding the abuse,
Life after death,
Change,
Years off your life.

To stop slavery,
13th Amendment,
Sentence reform,
Overpopulating prisons.

Families,
Understanding,
Life's focus,
Elderly abuse.

The sick,
Medical needs,
Truths,
A member of society.

If you're not a murderer,
We won't help you.

WASHINGTON'S DOC, BUDGET & DECARCERATION

The facts:
Washington State Department of Corrections (DOC) has a annual budget of over one billion dollars. The biggest budget in Washington State is for prisons.
Which includes:
Operating Prisons (electricity, etc)
> $599 million

Staffing
> $ 63.8 million

Programming
> $ 62 million

Healthcare
> $175 million

Our prisons are currently overcrowded due to over incarceration! DOC wants to build a new women's prison, expand Work Release and other expansion projects but has no plans to actually reduce the prison population through release. According to prisoners inside, social distancing for Covid 19 is not, or rarely, happening. Instead, DOC is proposing expanding medical facilities.

Due to Covid 19, Washington State is facing a budget deficit of $9 billion over the next 3 years. They cut all major programs that would benefit the incarcerated: Chemical Dependency and so on.

Major slashes:
40,000 state employees will be furloughed one day a week through the fall.
$310 million from the higher education system.
$2.1 million from the Dept of Health's reproductive health programs, which would mean over 16,000 people would lose access to necessary health care.

As of January 2019, Washington State had an estimated 21,577 experiencing homelessness on any given day. Of those, 1585 were Veterans; 1911 were unaccompanied young adults (aged 18-24). 4,884 were individuals experiencing chronic homelessness.

What does this mean for Washington? DOC is not proposing any cuts that would actually ease overcrowding, keep prisoners safe during Covid 19, or reduce the ballooning prison population. We cannot build our way out of overcrowding! We must cancel all future construction and expansion plans and put a moratorium on any new prisons.

Any response to reducing overcrowding and budget cuts should focus on releasing prisoners. In addition, DOC should reduce staffing, close empty prisons and facilities, and turn over re-entry and recidivism programming to community-based organizations that provide healthy community alternatives to incarceration.

Covid 19 saved Washington State. Washington State was so in debt, somewhere around $8 million. They were to lay off DOC employees and close down prisons. When Covid 19 hit.

Bidden, our President, gave Washington State millions of dollars. Washington State would take the money and tell our government it cost this much, when it didn't. Three times more, and what they did with it nobody knows. They kept putting us incarcerated into segregation and gyms and tents instead of letting us stay in our cells where it was safe! Way after Covid was gone, DOC would put the tents up in the parking lots. As long as they were up, they were getting paid. They raked in millions, and still nobody knows where the money went.

The prisons they said were closing down, is a lie. They call it "soft closing", but they will leave a full population of DOC employees there, and a handful of inmates to keep it running. So, the taxpayers are paying for supposedly empty prisons with the full staff of a regular prison. They receive overtime for doing nothing. They're still charging the state full electric bills, water and so forth, when there's not supposed to be anybody there. The inmates keep everything going and they're not supposed to be there.

This is so they can re-open the prisons again. They never laid off any DOC staff; none of the money went into medical where our health is neglected; no programs; we have very little movement and always in our cells. As you read my poems you will see how lazy all DOC employees are. They do nothing. And our taxpayers don't know where any of that budget goes. They don't spend it on the incarcerated.

I am working with advocates of as many states I can get ahold of, so I can add to my poems, to what's really going on around the U.S.

The incarcerated can't correspond to the incarcerated in Washington State, so you can have your families, prison advocates contact me. I'll add your voice to my books. I want everyone around the U.S. to know what's really going on in our prison system, and how we are being treated.

You can get a hold of me through

Email: www.securustech.net
Name: John Steiner #245917
Washington State
Prison: Twin River Unit

Or, through my publisher.

ALL THE WAY TO THE BANK

Lock us down,
Screw down the vents,
Turn up the heat,
Spread the germs that we don't need.
Everyone negative,
Now positive.
The more money we make,
The happier we'll be.
Second class people, we know they don't count.
Our Governor is the best,
Less the Feds know, they're better off,
As we laugh all the way to the bank.
Let them die, we have many in waiting.
Thank God for prisons,
All the way to the bank

COVID-19 SURVIVOR

DOC is telling the Feds they're spending this much on
Covid,
When they're not,
And the Feds will reimburse the State,
So, they're getting three to four times,
On what they spent.

COVID SLEEP DOWN

Strike me hard, turn me around,
Pick me up, change my world.
Whip away my tears, show me the new way.
They say a dose a day,
Will keep the doctor away.

Are you smiling?
I can't see.
Just to be held for a day,
It would be like that first kiss,
Which is only a memory.

You're here one day, gone the next.
Where did everybody go.
Don't touch me, stay away.
Millions of the old are gone,
But the ageless are being born every day.
Gone with the old, in with the new,
It is the new way, and it's just not for a day.

COVID-19

Runny nose, blood shot eyes,
Lack of breath to my surprise.
The tasteless days and nights,
I toss and turn without delight.

COVID SAVED DOC

We lost our hate supporters,
We lost our funds,
To carry out our evil ways.

We have to close prisons,
When we want more,
$800 million in debt.

We are crying,
Because we are losing our evil ways,
The only place we can be who we are.

To crack the whip,
Where will we go, what will we do?
Nobody will hire a DOC employee.

We don't want anything to do with work,
Where can we hurt people and nobody cares,
Oh, oh God has shined down on us.

He must be as evil as we are,
He brought us Covid.
The Feds pay us, the State pays us.

Double time, triple time, hazard pay,
And we are as evil as ever, if not more.
The Feds paid our debt.

More prisons, more prisons,
We make more money than the police.
We are going to be rich; we are going to be rich.
Thank God for Covid.

COVID SEGREGATION

With a turnoff a stick, 99.9 false positives,
With the Rapid Test that line their pockets,
Shackled and masked.
Piled into a hot metal box.

To go out of the prison for 3 blocks to the next prison,
Now I'm being punished, the door slides shut,
Without a slot for consumables.
The walls are oozing of human leftovers.

Sanitation, indigestion,
Isolation, simulation.
Laziness is a inbred, help is a lost art.
Out of sight out of mind.

Cold food in a paper box, protein is a lost cause,
If you could cry it would only be bubbles,
coming from the bottom of the ocean.
The medical help all wear badges.

If they took away their media,
Their lives would crumble.
Communication is done by two cans and a string.
Sickness is a death sentence.

As the heart worries,
There is no care, only money.
As I look out my hole,
There is need for Sono Bello.

GENERATIONS

No new blood,
No new ways,
Generations of hate.

Learn from your mistakes,
That will never take place,
$5700 per person.

We can't tell,
No new blood,
No new ways.

Generations of hate,
Learn from your mistakes,
That will never take pictures.

$5700 per person,
We can't tell,
Where it went.

Nobody knows,
Still hungry,
Still cold.

THEY BLAME COVID ON US

They come in, they go out,
They come in, they go out,
They go to bars, stores, concerts,
They laugh, play, and eat.

No masks, no worries,
They will pretend to wear masks when they come in,
They will work in a quarantined area,
And life is grand.

Now sick in one place, sick in another,
With no cares, no worries,
They blame us, they blame us,
When they come and go.

Soon as the gate opens,
Their masks are off, their cars running,
They smile as they pat their wallets,
Knowing this will never end.

So life for us is a solitary one,
As our governor lines his pockets,
And everyone gets to go home,
And start all over again.

Now Covid is our lifetime,
and nobody else's,
It's a one-way disease,
Wondering why us.

But money affects the greedy,
And I haven't seen a smile in years.

AS OF JANUARY 2024

This is what's going on in Washington State, as of 1-24, in male prisons. They are taking straight males' rights away to choose. They are letting women who identify as men to strip males, not allowing them to choose a male-born male. If you don't let them do this, you will get a write-up. And if you refuse to be stripped by this person, you won't be able to go to your outside medical appointment, which is badly needed by most of us because of the poor health DOC has put us in!

I believe everyone should have choices and rights, no matter who they are. But in Washington State, they are taking our rights away to choose and is only one-sided. This is against the 14th Amendment. This is causing a lot of trouble with poor health, beliefs, and the removing of your rights.

People are dying and the prisons are getting worse, not better. I am sure this is probably going on in California and other states. On the streets, this would be considered rape where consent wasn't given. And again, we have no rights. We are slaves.

CORE

CORE is a training program that trains Department of Corrections employees how to protect themselves. They teach you how to abuse incarcerated individuals physically and mentally. That a DOC employee is right no matter what. They tell their DOC employees that the incarcerated have no rights!

Even when you're wrong, or even when you kill an incarcerated person. Your protected by The Union! It's very seldom a DOC employee gets fired. They just keep moving you to another institution, and eventually, Headquarters. DOC headquarters take care of their employees even if they're wrong, which there is no accountability. They just promote you!

It's a "good ol' boys" club. Mostly families, fathers, mothers, brothers, sisters, wives, lovers, and friends. If you're not a good ol' boy, or a friend or family, they use scare tactics, put you in a job that no one wants until you quit.

Our system is broken, but nobody knows, and nobody cares.

WANTED DOC

No education, no resume,
Haters wanted.
Take our CORE and hate more,
Never have to work a day in your life.

Sit and surf the Web all day,
You only have to get up and walk every hour.
If you like looking in windows and showers,
We want you.

Never worry, no accountability,
You're right no matter what,
You don't have to be in shape, overweight, the better.
All the overtime you want.

That bank account will build up,
And there's no need to work.
You will have many friends that are like you.
You can do what you want.

Free food, free drinks, all the donuts you can eat.

If you're from another country,
Come work for us,
You will have your Green Card in two years.

You can hurt people and not have to worry,
Do things wrong and get promoted,
Never worry, we got your back,
Play with cuffs and chains all day.

Curse and swear,
A dream come true.

CI

We don't care about you,
You are slaves so true,
Many to take your place.
When life is so blue,
Millions of dollars a year,
And pennies for you.

IF WE HAD A WHIP

You can't eat anything,
That is opened or damaged,
You are our slaves so true,
We give it away and don't care about you.

You slave hard all day,
And we feed the hogs,
Better than we feed you.

Peanut butter sandwich for breakfast,
And peanut butter for lunch,
And you're lucky to get that.

We make millions thanks to our slaves,
Who work so hard,
No incentives,
If only we had a whip.

EDUCATION

Professors, teachers, a thing of the past,
All imposters,
All wear badges.
We don't care about you.

You don't show up, we write you up,
Sixty- and seventy-year-olds,
You have to get your GED,
Crippled and blind.

We don't care,
Failed to follow a direct order,
Failed to program,
We take your release points.

Again, we wear badges,
We are not teachers,
We get paid by the head,
Pile them in.

All new classes same as the old classes,
We change the name,
More money, more money.

Scare tactics,
Keep the real teachers out,
And you here.

GRIEVANCE

Write the wrongs,
DOC hires DOC,
To write the wrongs,
Union wages.

To govern themselves,
Physical, mental, verbal,
Three levels of Nos!
Lies and laughs.

They say we don't do that,
The higher ups back them up,
Three level of lies,
DOC WAC rules.

Even when wrong,
There right,
DOC WAC rules,
Made for them.

Kill, maim, abuse,
Finger cramps,
Writing all three levels,
Of Nos.

Can't get help,
The state don't care,
When wrong,
They hide their wrongs.

NO DREAMS

Wanted haters for hire,
Take our CORE and hate more.
Mental, physical, it's all fun,
No life's ambition,
No dreams.
That's why I work here.

Every night the bottle drops,
A shot before work,
One eye in the morning,
One eye in the evening.

Families and friends have a life of their own,
My loneliness is dreams of work.
Where I see my friends and families,
Stories how we hurt and abuse.
With each sunset, like a turn of a page.

Average life span after retirement,
Five years and no missed tears.

I LOVE MY JOB

I rise at the crack of dawn,
Another great day of nothing.
The smell of coffee and the wrongs I can do.

Sixteen hours of internet, streaming movies,
Facebook and shopping.
Shaping a lifetime of sitting.

Get up every hour just to take a walk,
If I can lock them down all day,
And not have to walk.

I love my job.

GAMES PEOPLE PLAY

No programs, no jobs.
Treated with hate and disrespect.
Restless and bored,
Hard to occupy your time.

Young and inexperience,
Irritation with smiles.
Not knowing what to do,
Fights with no meanings.

No yard, no nothing.
Locked down, nowhere to go,
Treat them with hate,
Lock them down.

No worries, don't have to work,
All the money we make,
With all the money they take,
With lost hope and tears.

DO YOU WANT A JOB

Do you want a job?
For friends and families.
Do you want a job?
To reap the bennies.

Do you want a job?
Doing nothing.
Do you want a job?
You can be in medical or corrections.

Do you want a job?
No education, no qualifications.
Do you want a job?
To be with your mom, brother, sister, dad, boyfriend.

Do you want a job?
All you got to do is fake it.
Do you want a job?
It's all old school.

Do you want a job?
You're right, no matter what.
Do you want a job?
So what if you kill a few.

Do you want a job?
You're with family.
Do you want a job?
And they don't care.

Do you want a job?
Lucky you.

Do you want a job?
You can't do this nowhere else.

Do you want a job?
Lucky you.
Welcome to the good ol' boy club.
No place on earth like it.

SHIFT CHANGE

During shift change you will meet evil.
You will feel the cold,
And a chill to the bone.
With a heart that never beats,
As high fives are met.
With their sinister smiles and a wink.

And we are nearing the journey's end.
Where time and eternity meet and blend.
Concrete and steel,
My heart still bleeds.

Behind the gate, another world,
Nobody knows.
The torturing of souls,
Blind and deaf,
In the light of the day.
I have seen the devil's face.

DOC FIRING RANGE

Thunder outside the walls every day.
The smiles with hate and discontent,
Dreams to do their wants.
Soured hearts with dreams of death.

The same hate and discontent,
Leaves them outside the gates.
Who are you? Why?
The hate of humanity.

Should society fear; should we cry?
Will my kids be alright?
Why are we hated?
With the smiles being above the law.

You say you're right, know matter what.
No countability, we're above the law.
We're right- we're always right,
Our hearts fill with joy.

For we get paid for doing what we love,
The tears, the broken families,
Light our hearts.
The joy of life is ours.

I'M NOT LIKE THEM

You say you are good.
You see what they are doing,
And how they are treating us.

You say you're not like them,
But yet you don't say anything.
Stop! Don't do that! You say nothing.

Yet again you say you are a good person.
While all this is going on,
You smile and laugh with them.

You are friends with them.
After work your kids play with their kids,
But yet again you say you're not like them.

And again, you say nothing.
You are as bad as the people,
That are treating us this way.

Or worst,
Because you lie about yourself,
And yet again, you say you are a good person.

Yet money talks,
Lives are broken,
Life goes on

DOC FIRING RANGE

Outside every fence and walls of prisons across America, they have firing ranges where they're trained to kill. You hear the firing of bullets seven days a week. I've seen inmates, by hearing this, has caused anxiety, PTSD and paranoia, and leaves a person scared.

These DOC employees they train are young and haven't fired a gun or even hunted. DOC is going to schools and fairs to recruit them saying a career in corrections is where it's at. Trying to keep the good ol' boy system going! Praising them and telling them there's no worries. What I've been seeing for years is correctional officers while at work living on the computer, looking and buying the best guns that can kill a person. Again, they're not hunting rifles. You can hear them talk on how bad they want to shoot someone to kill them!

Here's a quick story that I've at one of the prisons I was at. This inmate, for some reason, decided to jump in this small truck and tried to run through four fences, in which he knew was impossible. He hit one fence, the truck stopped and wouldn't go any more. The inmate got out. There was still four fences to go before he could even think about escaping. Razor wire and all. So, what happened was before you knew it, the corrections officers had rifles, the inmate wasn't going anywhere but the corrections officers shot him dead. The sad thing was what the corrections officers did next, they gave each other "high fives" and the next day they celebrated by having a BBQ for the staff for killing this person.

They used the money to have the BBQ from the Inmate Betterment Fund, which is only for the inmates. They do that all the time, and they have been caught!

Another example of incompetence and putting guns into the wrong hand. In 1971, the prison riot at Attica State Prison in New York. It was about race, class, power, prison reform and the poor conditions in the prison. Where the inmates were beaten every day. This caused a revolt where many correctional officers and inmates were killed. After the bodies were checked, the majority of the corrections officers killed were by their own bullets. Again, look who is given the guns to. It's the incompetence of the Governors across America. Guns should be in the hands of "only" military and police who have years of experience, not the Department of Corrections and the Good Ol' Boy system where incompetence, and death, is a everyday cover-up. There's over two million people in prison in the United States that will not see the sky at night, and not know if they will wake up the next morning.

BURIED OUT BACK

Lonely and forgotten,
Old and abused,
The dirt piles up.
Slipped through the cracks.

Never alone in the company of lost souls,
Six feet deep,
No where to go.
No family, no friends.

Time has ran out,
The mistreatment has lifted,
Time to go home.
Never alone.

ALONE

Alone is a quiet place,
The heart pounds but nobody hears it.
The tears fall but nobody sees it.

Hope is just hope,
The walls are closing in.
There's no light, only darkness.

It's like seeing the stars,
But only a void of the mind.
It's like being the last person on earth.

With no one to say hello to,
Here they say a laugh is your friend,
As the mind fades into memory.

Soon the soul will fly,
The pain will fade,
And alone no more.

DOC FIRING RANGE

Every day, seven days,
The lightning strikes the soul.
Our hearts are lined up side by side,
Wondering who's who,
And when?

You say you become use to it,
Until your day comes.
I feel like it's ever day,
And not a day passes.

I can feel the bullets,
As they pierce my soul.
The training of death,
Is a sinister one.

Feelings are nowhere around,
And it's not their hearts
That guide them.
As I look around.

BROKEN EARS

If you can see the abuse that I see,
Through my neon eyes,
The sadness that is in my body-bag eyelids.

Droop with tears of a stroke,
That pains me deep inside,
With the promises of lies.

No left turns, only rights,
Hoping to find the crossroads.
They listen to me with broken ears.

The map is only one way.
There's only one door in or out,
But the out is always locked.

The future is paid for,
With money in their pockets.
Life is one way and greed for the other.

WE WILL MISS YOU

When death comes,
No matter what side,
The heart cries,
The world stops.

The rainbow comes and goes,
The things that numbs the heart,
If I could give you my breath,
I would.

If I could stop one heart from breaking,
Or feel one's pain,
Or help one lonely person,
Into happiness again.

Why should anyone be glad,
When another heart is sad,
A family's lost,
A father's love.

If you see the tears falling,
From a brother's eyes,
Share them,
Hug them.

The smile and your sense of humor,
When there was no hope,
If I can shake your hand.
We will miss you.

NO HUMANITY

As I walk with death,
The blackness I can see,
As the body decays.

Hope and death is the same.
I'm hoping for the Journey's end.
I'm told lies as each day ends.

My body is as light as my soul.
With my last breath,
I hold myself tight.

DOC won't let me die,
In my family's arms.
To the last penny they will take.

Your sentence isn't done,
Until you're dead and gone,
With a smile they will say.

Everything will be OK,
As they hide you away,
Forgotten and alone.

There is no humanity,
Only insanity,
As cancer kills us all.

They are the cancer.
The evil spreads,
As the tears water my grave.

CONDEMNED MAN

I gone out, a condemned man,
Haunting the cold air, hiding in the daylight,
Dreaming of old memories, wondering if there is a hitch.
Over the plain cell a reflected light shines.
Loneliness is a out-of-mind thing.
A man like that can only hope.
I have been his kind.

I have found a warm blanket in the corner of the cell,
Filled with filth and six-legged brothers.
I share my crumbs with my four-legged cell mates.
While deep in conversation,
A man like that is misunderstood.
I have been his kind.

I have dragged the rusted chains,
As I am followed by the many lost souls.
You try to dodge the words thrown by the villagers.
My thighs are still bitten by the flames,
As the wheels crack my ribs.
The wind still blows in my head.
I have been his kind.

ABUSE

Straight killed, death by execution.
Faster, better, quicker.
Better than a lifetime of abuse,
Or even a short time of abuse.

No matter what crime,
Humans are not made for torture.
Mental, physical, it's all a crime.
A quick death better than a white lie.

Still wondering why people are committing suicide?
Your taxes pay for the abuse.
Does anybody know? Does anybody care?
Still crying over slavery, and it's still going on.

Does anybody know? Does anybody care?
Never see it in the news, and never will.
Hidden secrets, eyes closed, no smiles,
Only tears.

Daisies in the future.

FAILED UPWARD

Washington state correctional system is broken like all of them around the U.S., and they don't want to change. Mass money is made from prisons. Taxpayers and money-making programs, and the thanks belong to the governor!

The Department of Correction's majority they hire are not qualified for their positions. Our governor hires the Director of Prisons to run all of the prisons. The Director of Prisons was once CEO of Western State Hospital and was promoted to the Department of Social and Health, in which both was failed in. From there he was promoted to the Director of Prisons. The director said change is on its way, "We are going to have prison reform and be more humane to the incarcerated". Nothing has changed and things have gotten worse.

When Department of Corrections employees fail, instead of firing them when they get into trouble, they fail upwards. The worse they get, the more promotions they get. When they're just plain bad, they get promoted to Headquarters with more pay and nobody knows what happened to them, and they get to make the rules to continue the abuse. That goes on in all prisons. This is happening around the U.S. They fail upwards.

CRY

Do you cry?
Yes, I cry,
I cry for you,
And I cry for me.

I cry for my children,
I cry for the lies,
And I cry for the truths.
I cry for the kindness.

And I cry for the meanness,
I cry for the happiness,
And I cry for the sadness.
I cry for the lovers.

I cry for the haters,
And I cry with all my heart.

I AM RIGHT HERE

Hello, hello, do you see me?
I am right here.
I try to talk,
But nobody listens.

I try to listen,
But nobody talks.
I see you,
But you don't see me.

I try to laugh,
But only cry.
I know you're there,
Even when you say you're not.

I hear the whispers,
I feel the tears.
I wonder if I'm the only one.

ABUSE

Corrupt practice,
Coarse and insulting speech.
Mistreatment,
Every day, all day.

They will lie and say it's not true.
When your life is so blue,
No one cares and no one knows.
Just another day.

It's a nightmare that nobody knows.
Every day is in the dark,
There's no light at the end of the tunnel.
Dreams that never come true.

WE DID NOTHING

They come in deep as the ocean.
The waves crash,
The bubbles float to the top.
The sound of thunder,
As the rain pours,
The birds use to sing,
As the nights are silent.

PAROLE BOARD

There are many gods,
Mine has the power of freedom or death.
Their names are not known,
But they are gods of pain and misery.

Tears have no effect on the dead.
A bad day for them is a bad day for you.
Freedom is not in their demise.
Hates is their kingdom, they rule with hate.

To be released to heaven,
Would show weakness and less rule.
With the inflicted pain and misery,
They gain their strength and pleasure.

We do not have a choice.
We are slaves to their kingdom.
Our lives are eternal to suffering.
Their fires will burn forever in our soul.

MEDICAL

Medical in prisons around the U.S. is bare minimum to none existing. Their medical records are paper, not digitalized, so outside doctors can't look up your health issues. The reason for this is that paper records can be lost or changed, and as you age and have done a lot of time, your paper files grow to large amounts.

DOC have been sued so many times for neglect. They use the taxpayers' money to retain lawyers (this is full-time). DOC drags out court cases for many years. It's why the incarcerated settle out of court. The problem is the majority of medical staff don't qualify for their jobs. They're just wives and friends of correctional officers and other DOC employees. They have no medical training whatsoever. If they do have medical training, they were fired from hospitals with blemished records and can't work in the medical field!

This is a regular thing! DOC will teach you how to take blood pressures and temperatures and you're good to go. The medical staff that hand out the medication are not pharmacists, and hands out the wrong medication, usually someone else's. This has happened to me and has hurt me. Again, not qualified.

I was at this one prison and there were two DOC doctors there, and prisoners were being neglected and hurt. We had a lawyer look these doctors up. One couldn't practice in Washington State, and the other was a veterinarian. Once they were found out, they were gone. This is happening through the U.S. Just killing the incarcerated.

DOC doesn't care if you die, there's many prisoners waiting to come to prison from the jails, so it's cheaper to let you die and pay the lawsuits. I was sitting in a waiting room which is a cell of cheap plywood, waiting to see my provider. While waiting, this medical staff was telling this new person they hired, "You don't have to do anything. Just collect a paycheck!" How sad and scary for us.

SUICIDE

Lights flash,
The sweet smells,
The chill of ice,
The heat of the desert,
The feeling of ecstasy.
Reflections of the past,
Smiles with tears.
The shake of a earthquake,
The white light,
The feeling of home.

ADDICTION

The pain,
The tears in my eyes,
The misery, the pleasure.

The relief,
The numbness in my body,
Tomorrow? Scared.

Looking forward to another day,
Pain, pleasure.
When will it stop.

Will there be another day?

LIFE IS SHORT

As I am being looked down on,
I feel the size of a ant,
As the foot sets upon me,
Since we're so close to the ground.

And you see yourself the Sun.
Shines on the other side of the world,
Growth is stunted,
And the wind blows.

The hollow feeling,
That the season will never change,
As I want to bloom.
The pedals fall.

There's only one kind of fruit,
Not like the other.
Life is short,
As I try to wash the rain from my eyes.

LOST HOPE AND SUICIDE

I have seen the loss of souls,
I felt the cries,
As my feet carry me through hell.

The smell of death is all around,
As another takes his life.
The walls have a history.

And you can hear what they say.
My mind goes numb with so much guilt.
To see what I've seen.

Wandering why I am still here,
And not the ones who have gone.
I still talk to them at night.

And I listen to their cries,
And I know I'll be one of them,
If not in death, in mind.

DOC FISHBOWL

My life is a circle.
I swim back n' forth, back n' forth,
No where to go.

I am alone.
I wait for crumbs and hope to survive another day.
I can see outside.

But can't go anywhere.
I'm looked at every day,
And wonder what they see.

Life expectancy isn't very long.
Soon the toilet will come,
And the flush will begin.

Many more to come,
Many more to go.
There will never be a end.

Always a beginning.
Always.

DOC MEDICAL

I hold myself while I cry inside.
I see the pain they just don't see.
There is no help or bedside manners,
They just smile and turn you away.

We know there's no help, and death is on its way.
It's cheaper to pay all the lawsuits,
When preventative help would help us all.
Life is short here, but nobody cares.

Here one day, gone the next.
Don't let anyone tell you we are all the same.
Color doesn't make a difference; they treat us all the same.

It's sunny in one place, cloudy in another.
You can see the hate in their eyes,
And the smiles in their heart.
When all we want is to see another day.

HOPE IS LIKE A ROSE

With a twist and a turn,
Life changes,
But the colors stay the same.

But the sun
Shines through the rain,
But the tears still fall.

The beauty is there,
If you can see through the dark.
Hope is like a rose,
The beauty will show.

But when winter sinks in,
The chill begins.
Life is only a beginning,
There is always a end.

PILL LINE

Wheelchairs, walkers, canes,
As I walk out the door,
The wind, rain, sun, snow, smoke.
The worst in the world.

Slaps me in the face, as I hold my breath.
As my legs shakes, the line is long.
As we get sicker waiting for our medicines.
Outside the suffering of cheap wet clothes.

Not understanding why?
We are getting our medication outside,
Not inside,
With the warmth everyone deserves.

But yet you are inside warm,
Giving us our medication.
My thoughts are freezing,
And the tears running down my face.

Life isn't easy,
Why as I cry.
Life isn't easy,
Is anyone wondering why?
Life isn't easy,
Why as I cry.

4TH FLOOR

DOC hospital,
Built in the 1800s,
Where time is not forgotten.

Cold and all alone,
Hidden from the world,
Locked in, out of sight.

Dreaming of the end,
Hoping to see the light.
Sorry for being alive.

Sick and froze to the bone,
The food is as cold as your heart.
Legal suicide.

When you get sick,
You go from minimum to closed.
From closed to the grave.

Concrete to bones,
10 blankets to hell.
Always alone.

One thing good,
Only thing good,
Closer to heaven.

FOOD

The food is so bad! It was proven that feeding the incarcerated real nutritional food was cheaper, but the governor before this one decided to turn prisons into a business and take everything away from the incarcerated, so the food is all in plastic bags steamed and boiled, and the food is bad!

The majority of the food is all carbs so it causes bad health issues like diabetes, heart problems, high blood pressure and much more. They throw tons of uneaten food out to show you how bad it is, but don't care because they're paying pennies for it and not caring if you eat or not!

They even fed us a food product that says "not fit for human consumption" on the box. The Department of Corrections has no sympathy for human life. The present governor hasn't changed a thing and continues to reap the benefits from the last governor.

CI

Boxes get broke,
Bags tore open.
Instead of feeding your workers,
You give it away.

The pennies you make,
The needs you buy,
It's a 300% mark up.
Where's the pride?

No hope with the billions they take,
And the lives they hurt,
Money is made from the lives they take.

DON'T DRINK THE WATER

Don't drink the water, don't drink the water,
The C/O's are told.
Drink our bottled water, drink our bottled water,
Or bring your own.

The towers are chemically infected.
It's OK, it's OK,
For the incarcerated to drink it,
But don't you, but don't you.

Your health will fail, your health will fail,
Then we would have to pay, we would have to pay.
It's OK, it's OK,
For the incarcerated to drink it.

Little do they know, little do they know,
The towers are chemically infected, chemically infected.
The governor knows, the governor knows.
It's OK, it's OK.

It's a big business, it's a big business.
Know matter how the incarcerated leaves,
Many more to come, many more to come.
We have many lawyers to appeal to no end.

Sooner or later, sooner or later,
They will settle, they will settle.
No worries, no worries,
Just another third world country.

Where the rich get richer, where the rich get richer,
And the poor get poorer.

CI FOOD

All carbs, no taste,
Protein a thing of the past.
Eat or go hungry.

Diabetes, poor health,
Death on the rise.
20 minutes, get up and go.

Each meal swallowed,
Not chewed.
Plates are dirty.

Taste like soap,
With no hope.
No fresh food all in a bag.

Plastic and boiled,
Where all is sad.
Old fish, not from the sea.

Correctional Industries,
Padding their wallet.
Not caring if you eat or die.

With many smiles along the way,
Peanut butter and jelly for breakfast.
Tomorrow, just another day.

POEMS FROM THE INNER SOUL

INNOCENT

You did this,
You did this,
You did this.

No, I didn't,
No, I didn't,
No, I didn't.

Say what you want,
Mean what you say.

Thinking and knowing,
Are two different things.

Lying hurts,
The truth heals,
The tongue kills.

And innocents prevail,
Home is on the hill.

PRETTY ON THE OUTSIDE

With so much eye candy,
The heart jumps.
The beauty of a lifetime.
The mountains point to the heavens.

As the oceans licking at the shores,
But the tears still fall.
Hate with discontent,
With silver bullets of death.

Every day, all day.
While each corner crumbles,
Tents of life stand,
Where homes should be.

Empty stomachs, babies crying,
Authority killing the minorities,
Of our beginnings,
Where all is equal.

Prisons on every corner,
With business of life.
The rich get richer.

While the highest taxes,
Strikes the poor and elderly.
Covie effects the poor,
While the power makes more.
No jobs, inflation takes us a foot.

As I look out my window,
With a smile and a tear,
The orcas are jumping,
Dragging their nets

Population falling,
As we lie to ourselves.
The sun is still shining,
As our heart crumble to the sea.

The mountains still beautiful,
With hope of a new day,
As the seagulls living off our throw-aways.

It's like looking through a keyhole.
Pretty on the outside.

I'D GIVE YOU MY HAND

I reach down inside,
You can only go so far.
It seems like birth was yesterday,
With each breath,
The heart beats.

I've been turned inside out,
With poison rules of the past,
Which is now the future.
The corruptions of the State,
Of Corrections.

Lost and confused,
Money for lives taken.
Would you treat me a poor man,
As you would a millionaire?
I haven't done anything this wrong,
To say I'm sorry.

I am sorry for the ones,
That are confused.
Where their hearts,
Have been punished as a child.
The values that have been lost.

In their head,
It's OK to express their abuse.
Where the needs of others,
Are forgotten.

I'd give you my hand,
If only you would take it.
What's in your past,
Is not always true.

Both lives can change,
But the abuse has to stop.
Stop the lies,
And let society know.

WE WANT YOU BACK

Nobody knows.
As the blankets are pulled over,
The tear drops still fall.
Out of sight, out of mind,
As the abuse strikes our soul.

In the cover of the night,
A crime that nobody knows,
As our governor and his friends,
Are lining their pockets,
The grass isn't growing.

Dollar signs for each and every one.
Monopoly in the dark,
While the sick get sicker,
And the greedy get richer,
You are only who we say you are.

And nobody else,
We want you to hate us,
We want you back.
More, the better,
No change, only dollars.

Empty promises,
No new starts.
The lights are turned off,
Still in the dark.

Modern day slavery,
Same as yesterday.
It's a certain kind of person,

To do what they do.
Don't look back, don't tell.

Hate is on the rise for the ones who wear blue,
Countability is for losers,
And fairness is a lost cause.
Yesterday, same as today,
Modern day slavery, same as yesterday.

AKA-RUGS

I wake up every morning on the floor,
I turn my head right I smell the toilet,
I turn my head left, the smell of bad breath.

I tiptoe to the right and to the left,
I jump over one, two, three,
Hello, excuse me, I'm sorry.

Just to use the bathroom.
No door, hello, I'm sorry, excuse me,
As I sit there.

I see angry eyes,
I feel like I want to cry,
Lack of privacy, to my demise.

A feeling no one should have to go through.
Overpopulated, mass incarceration,
Every day a dangerous day.

I roll up my mattress just to have a seat.
Five people in a 7.5 x 13.5 cell,
Life is a living hell.
Two beds and three rugs.

FORGOTTEN

There is a time when you are forgotten,
A age of life's lessons.
Out of sight, out of mind.

Memories of the past,
Lost to the future.
Destiny comes to every end.

And life goes on.
Your journey is what everyone takes,
No matter how many steps.

The young forget the old,
As memory fails.

THE WHOLE WORLD HAS THE BLUES

With every breath the world turns,
War and hate,
Confusion and disbelief.

Sunshine where it was cold,
Viruses with death,
The prejudice smiles.

The sickness turns the heart,
The tears of hunger,
The world cries, is religion real?

Brothers killing brothers,
Mental health only a dream,
The world turns upside down.

Warehousing the world,
Where greed profits.
The world is disappearing.

The thirst of life is gone,
But we're dreaming of other worlds.
Are we too late?

Take, take, take,
Do we have a chance or only a dream?
Is our thinking so constipated?

That we don't give life a chance?

HELP

Help is a need,
That everyone needs.
A hand up,
Isn't a handout.

Is hope help,
Is help hope?
Can a person dream,
Can I ask?

Will anyone listen?

DESTINY

Tomorrow's a new day,
Just like yesterday,
Life goes on.

I see in my dreams,
I laugh in my sleep,
Hoping to see.

I know where I want to go,
I know what I want to see,
They can try to keep me.

But my heart is free,
Standing in the crossroads,
Just flip a coin.

I miss you life,
I will go home,
I'll see you again.

I feel you breathing,
I know you're alive,
And I won't stop trying.

Hold my hand,
Everything will be ok,
Hold my hand.

I won't let go,
Until the end,
Hold my hand.

I'll see you in the end.

BEHIND THE BRICK WALL

Under the covers,
Tear drops fall,
Memories scatter like leaves.

In the darkness nobody knows,
The heart is like a rose,
The pain is like vein.

Whispers in the wind,
The night has ears,
Nobody sees.

The darkness has took over,
The pain begins,
Nobody knows.

And there's never a end.

I THINK I'M OK

Even when I don't do what you say,
When I ran away from the headlights,
I find I'm still here.
I think I'm OK.

Even when I don't do what you say,
Tomorrow's a new day,
I can't wait for tonight.
I think I'm OK, just another day.

You say my heart is in the right place,
Even when it's in a different space.
I think I'm OK.
Even when I don't do what you say.

No hard feelings, no bad vibes,
I'm happy to be back in your eyes.
I can't wait til the sun comes up,
There's no hard feelings.

When I'm about to start,
I can see the tunnel in the dark,
And I laugh with all my heart,
When I tripped and fell.

You made a big yell,
But I'll come back from hell,
And life will be like a spell.
I think I'm OK.

CONCRETE SOULS

Twisted colors,
Concrete lives,
Where darkness lies,
Dreams begin.

Tears gathered, hopes broken,
Solitary smiles.
Humanity in its mist,
Darkness is light and light is darkness.

Gone forgotten, myth betrayal,
Heart breaks, memories.
Life's gone forever,
Children, love, hopes.

Endless river of tears,
Sleepless nights that never end.
A ray of light is a love never forgotten.
I have a concrete soul.

And I have become one with life's twist.

RAZOR WIRE AND MOUNTAINS

With each footstep around the track,
The beauty that strikes the soul,
God's gift to us all,
An escape from reality.

The mountains and their untold secrets,
Brings hope.
An emotion that is rare, life's gift to us all,
As the sun glistens off the razor wire.

And the fences that keeps out hearts from escaping,
As I look forward to that moment each day.
The sights that are in my dreams,
A memory that is a start to my day.

With a storm that comes in each and every day,
When the weather clears and the storm is gone,
The sun reflexes off my smile,
A memory that will never leave.

And a hope for a new day.

YESTERDAY'S TOMORROW

Each day we start again,
A new day, a new tomorrow,
A yesterday's farewell.

A blink of a eye,
A smile or a cry,
From yesterday to today.

DEEP BREATHS

Tight knots,
Loose smiles,
Twisted hearts,
Deep breaths.

DREAMS

A feather floats in the wind like a dream,
Far, far away.
Over the mountains through my dreams,
Far, far away.
From my mind to the stars and back,
Around the world in seconds flat.

FOOTSTEPS

Short journeys, long journeys,
From the beginning to the end.
From cries to smiles,
From the living room floor.

To the mountains,
Life has brought me from a crawl to a sprint,
And around the world.
From barefoot to boots.

THE WHISTLE BLOWS

The whistle blows,
The track vibrates.
Hopes and dreams fly by.

OPPOSITE SEX

As I feel the stares at my back,
As the goosebumps that rise,
When the water is rinsed from my eyes,
I see a smile.

Ten steps to my cell, I see two eyes.
As I change, this is a forever thing.
And will never change.
We have no rights or says,
And life is a gaze.

Even though there is no yeahs,
You're supposed to think this is ok.
Yet if we were on the streets,
Another sentence yee would get,
But yet it is ok.

PHOTOGRAPHS & MEMORIES

Fires from below,
Tears from above,
Insanity within.

Moment of light,
Memory of dreams,
I have never known a night so black.

I welcome the memory,
And I shelter the pain,
A sunshine of time.

A minute of the past,
A tear from the heart,
A hope for the future.

FREEDOM

The door opens,
You take that first step.
Your eyes blink,
The world explodes.
Memory sets in,
Tears begin.

A NEW BEGINNING

I miss those nights when I was hollow,
When my heart was crying,
And the nights were silent,
My mind was divided.

Nightmares in the light of the day,
Send your dogs away,
As the master is at bay.

The cliffs crumble to the sea,
As the ripples of my mind,
Between the knotholes of my past,
The phoenix will rise.

SMILES

Hate reads the letter and throws it away,
Love picks it up and smiles.
Hate said the world will die,
Love just smiles.

I'LL MEET YOU THERE

What is right and what is wrong?
Is it our parents and society,
That teaches us this?

Do we really know,
You could live on the other side of the world,
And your right may not be my right.

Your wrong may not be my wrong,
Do we really know?
Somewhere between right and wrong.

I'll meet you there.

DIFFERENCES

You look like that,
I look like this.
You do it like that,
I do it like this.

I eat this, you eat that.
I'm this color,
And you are that color.
You breath my air

And I breath your air.
My baby was born,
And so was yours.
We both cried, and,

We both smiled.

INSIDE OUT

Holocaust, World War II, slavery,
Did I go back in time as I moved forward,
Confined to the past in the present.

Scars of the mind and body,
Where the past is reality,
As the river of tears turn red.

Hope is of the mind,
Torturing of souls that slip through time,
Chained to the past.

As time withers away,
Humanity is a word,
As the future is the past.

Hatred controls the now and then,
Silence is a dirty word.
Freedom is another word for hunger.

As insanity slips through the cracks,
Where time is pain,
Death is another man's heaven.

It's like taking a shower and never leaving,
Nobody knows.
Humanity turned inside out.

STATES

OF

CONFUSION

TEXAS CRAZY

Cowboy hats to chains,
Chains to whips,
Insanity breeds.

Death is a need,
The noose takes another friend,
As the guards smile as they watch.

High fives and laughs,
Cockroaches to bed bugs,
With hate of the devil.

Raped from both sides,
Scarlet tears,
Lost in the dark.

Daily suicide is a win,
Come in alive,
Leave dead.

Polunsky's hell,
As the needle calling my name
Hoping heaven isn't a lie.

ALABAMA'S CRYING

South plantation,
Pouring down rain,
Day of pain,
Piled in the back of a truck.

Sounds of chains,
As lightning strikes,
Tears in a straight line,
Rifles out every window.

As the heart breathes cotton,
As the watchers whip,
Mud puddles of tears,
As the rain washes the blood off.

Where peace is sleep,
Smiles of dreams,
Where death is home,
And God is a lie.

Dogs are barking,
Licking their chops,
Hungry and cold,
No where to go.

Songs of the Blues,
To get you through.
We are us,
And you are you.

Overcrowded,
Hard to breathe,
Two steps to the south,
My babies are crying.

Boll weevils and grits,
Two biscuits left.
Lost and forgotten,
One breath to go.

The south once beautiful,
Now just dangerous.
I loved once,
But time is never forgotten.

I will remember,
I won't forget.
I'll never pray.
Alabama's crying.

THE BIG APPLE'S LIES

Concrete to concrete,
Skyscrapers to dungeons.
Enemy of my enemy,
Is my friend.

New York Jets,
To the Big Yard Kings,
Broadway to Attica,
Where they blame us for breathing.

Central Park to Cell Block 5,
Ten throats cut,
Fifty years of lies.
Bullets by their own.

Suffering in every corner,
Over 500 law enforcement agents,
Troopers and ex-prison guards,
Whatever.

Rifles, shot guns, tear gas,
Anyone, everyone,
Over and over again,
Fourth of July all over.

Nine minutes, thirty-nine killed,
The yard ran red.
Lifetime of pain,
As the rain pours.

Twelve million dollars,
Twenty-five years later,
Never the same,
And the media lies.

A famous person said this:

"Go to any prison during shift change, and you will see the worse of the worse."

I wrote this book by hand because DOC/Union Supply charges $474.95 for a typewriter which is obsolete on the streets and should be in here too!

That makes it over 400% mark-up! Again, we have no rights, and you are lucky to find a typewriter in a pawn shop.

INDEX OF POEMS

Covid Saved DOC

Covid Segregation

Generations

They Blame Covid on Us

Wanted DOC

CI

If We Had a Whip

Education

Grievance

No Dreams

I Love My Job

Games People Play

Do You Want a Job

Shift Change

DOC Firing Range

I'm Not Like Them

Buried Out Back

Alone

DOC Firing Range

Broken Ears

We Will Miss You

No Humanity

Condemned Man

Abuse

Cry

I am Right Here

Abuse

We Did Nothing

Parole Board

Suicide

Addiction

Life is Short

Lost Hope & Suicide

DOC Fishbowl

Texas Crazy

Alabama's Crying

The Big Apple's Lies

106

Made in United States
Troutdale, OR
11/07/2024